THE
WHITEBOARD
BIBLE®

VOLUME 1

FROM
CREATION
TO
KINGS

Allen Jackson

PASTOR, WORLD OUTREACH CHURCH

allenjackson.com

© 2015 by Allen Jackson for *The Whiteboard Bible Vol. 1: From Creation to Kings*. First edition 2014. Revised edition 2015.

The Whiteboard Bible® by Allen Jackson Ministries

Published by Allen Jackson Ministries
1921 New Salem Road, Hwy. 99
Murfreesboro, TN 37128

Special Sales:
Most Allen Jackson Ministries books are available at special quantity discounts when purchased in bulk by corporations, organizations, and special-interest groups. Custom imprinting or excerpting can also be done to fit special needs. For more information, please email: contact@allenjackson.com.

Illustrations: Imago
Design: Tommy Owen

ISBN: 978-1-61718-024-8

THE WHITEBOARD BIBLE®

FROM CREATION TO KINGS

CONTENTS

APPENDIX

SMALL GROUP LEADERS

ABOUT THE AUTHOR

INTRODUCTION

The Bible is a collection of sixty-six books. Many different authors contributed to the work. It was written in different cultural settings over a period of hundreds of years. The books are not arranged in chronological order. The names seem unusual, and the places are mostly unknown. It is not surprising that most Christians do not understand the Bible. We typically settle for a verse that offers comfort or hope and imagine that in a handful of verses we have the essence of this remarkable book.

The Bible tells a story. The amazing narrative begins with creation and concludes with Jesus triumphant. Between Genesis and Revelation is the story of God's interaction with the descendants of Adam. The Bible is not intended to be a science book or a history book. It is possible to gain historical insight from reading the Bible and even to understand our world better. The primary objective is to provide the reader insight into Almighty God and His interactions with the descendants of Adam.

Often, we avoid reading the Bible thinking it is simply too complex or boring. The Whiteboard Study has been designed to help anyone gain a fundamental understanding of the narrative of the Bible. Inside the books of the Bible are amazing accounts of men and women whose lives were transformed by God. The Bible unfolds a revelation of God that invites all readers toward hope and purpose.

Through three volumes we will develop a twelve-point timeline that will serve as the framework for all the characters and events in the Bible. We will take a journey from creation through the emergence of the Hebrew people. We will hear the prophets and listen to the Sadducees challenge Jesus. By the time the Whiteboard study is complete, we will be able to recount the progression of the biblical events in a simple, sequential order.

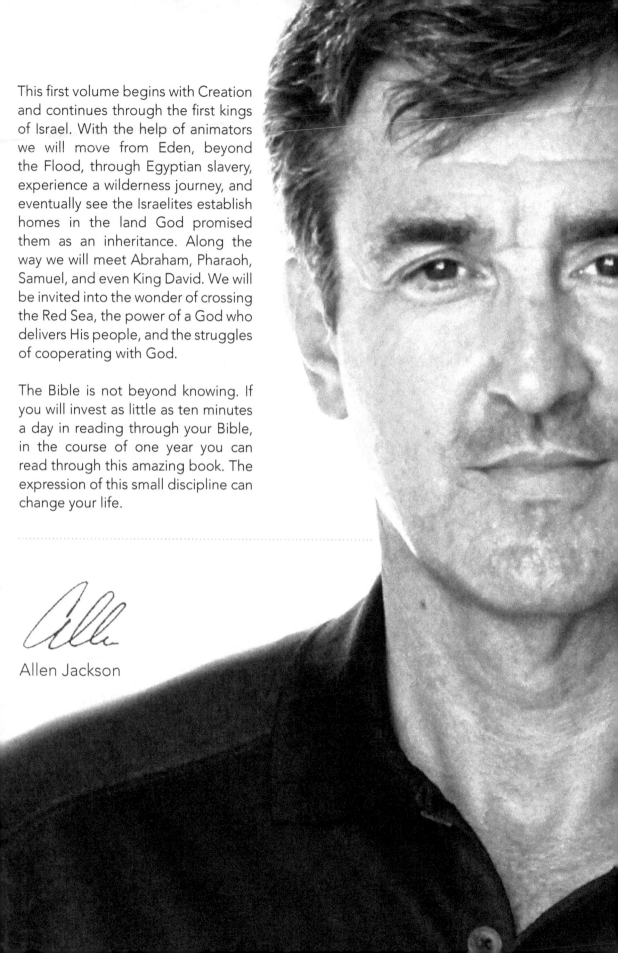

This first volume begins with Creation and continues through the first kings of Israel. With the help of animators we will move from Eden, beyond the Flood, through Egyptian slavery, experience a wilderness journey, and eventually see the Israelites establish homes in the land God promised them as an inheritance. Along the way we will meet Abraham, Pharaoh, Samuel, and even King David. We will be invited into the wonder of crossing the Red Sea, the power of a God who delivers His people, and the struggles of cooperating with God.

The Bible is not beyond knowing. If you will invest as little as ten minutes a day in reading through your Bible, in the course of one year you can read through this amazing book. The expression of this small discipline can change your life.

Allen Jackson

OUTLINE OF EACH SESSION

A typical group session for *The Whiteboard Bible* will include the following:

GETTING STARTED. The foundation for spiritual growth is an intimate connection with God and His family. A few people who really know you and who earn your trust provide a place to experience the life Jesus invites you to live. Using the icebreaker questions enables you to connect with one or two in your group to begin the discussion with ease.

DVD TEACHING SEGMENT. Serving as a companion to *The Whiteboard Bible* small group study guide is *The Whiteboard Bible* video teaching. This DVD is designed to present unique illustrations from the whiteboard and helpful teaching segments from Pastor Allen Jackson.

DISCUSSION. This section is where you will process as a group the teaching from the DVD. We want to help you apply the insights from Scripture practically, creatively, and from your heart as well as your head. Allowing the timeless truths from God's Word to transform our lives in Christ is our greatest aim.

APPLICATION. The objective of Bible study is not primarily information but transformation. Each week we will walk through questions intended to help us not only learn but apply what we have learned to our daily life.

DEEPER BIBLE STUDY. If you have time and want to dig deeper into more Bible passages about the topic at hand, we've provided additional passages and questions. Your group may choose to do homework after each meeting in order to cover more biblical material. If you prefer not to do homework, the Going Deeper section will provide you with plenty to discuss within the group. These options allow individuals or the whole group to expand their study, while still accommodating those who can't do homework or are new to your group.

DAILY DEVOTIONALS. Each week on the Daily Devotionals pages we provide scriptures to read and reflect on between group meetings. We suggest you use this section to seek God on your own throughout the week. This time at home should begin and end with prayer. Don't get in a hurry; take enough time to hear God's direction.

WEEKLY MEMORY VERSES. For each session we have provided a Memory Verse that emphasizes an important truth from the session. Memorizing Scripture can be a vital part of filling our minds with God's will for our lives. We encourage you to give this important habit a try.

READ ALOUD. Inside the Application and Discussion sections are additional teaching components to use with your group. These sections are a natural way to set up more dialogue for the questions that follow and also serve as a great tool for opening discussion in your group.

WEEK 1

INTRODUCTION

Welcome to *The Whiteboard Bible*, a way of picturing God's Word so we can understand the scope and sequence of the events through which God has worked since He created the world. As we will see in this Timeline Overview, it is possible to learn a simple timeline for the Bible that gives us a framework where we can fit all the stories, people, and lessons of Scripture. Once we see the big story unfolding, we can understand better how the various parts fit in God's plan. You can get this! In the weeks to come

THE BIG PICTURE

we will unpack each major point on the timeline so you will grow in your understanding of God's Word. We want to get to the place where the Bible is much more than a series of disconnected stories or familiar phrases. We want to "see" the Bible as an epic panorama that makes sense because we know the Author and because we can see the pattern He built into His story.

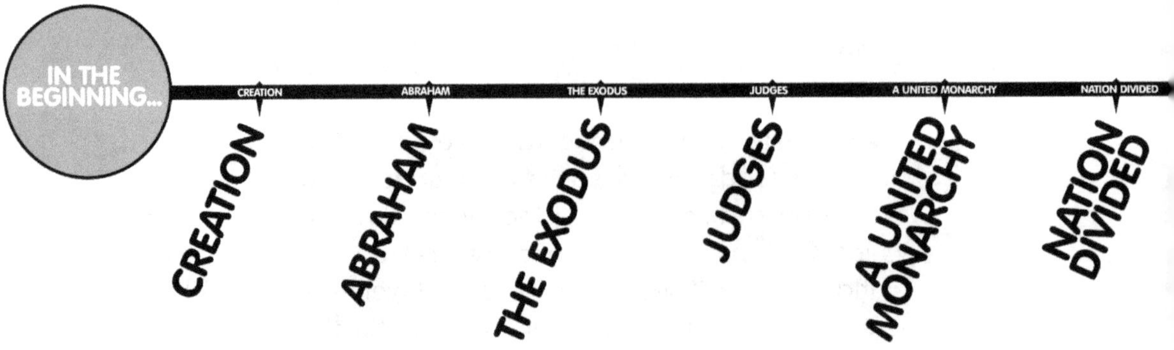

IN THE BEGINNING...
CREATION
ABRAHAM
THE EXODUS
JUDGES
A UNITED MONARCHY
NATION DIVIDED
CREATION
ABRAHAM
THE EXODUS
JUDGES
A UNITED MONARCHY
NATION DIVIDED

GETTING STARTED

Begin the session with a question below or brief activity to become better acquainted with one another. Then take a minute to introduce yourself to those in the group.

1 Do you have a favorite Bible story you would like to share with the group?

2 What is your preference: reading a book or watching a movie?

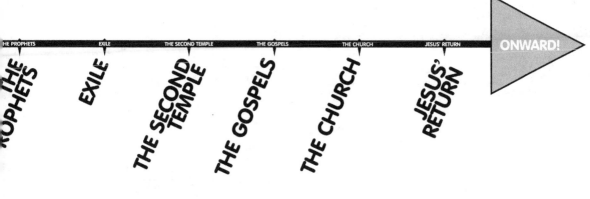

THE PROPHETS   EXILE   THE SECOND TEMPLE   THE GOSPELS   THE CHURCH   JESUS' RETURN   ONWARD!

THE PROPHETS

EXILE

THE SECOND TEMPLE

THE GOSPELS

THE CHURCH

JESUS' RETURN

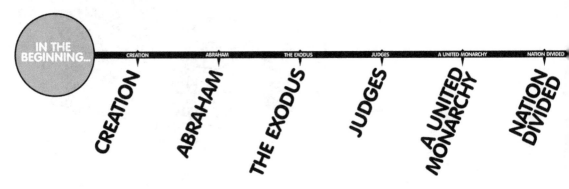

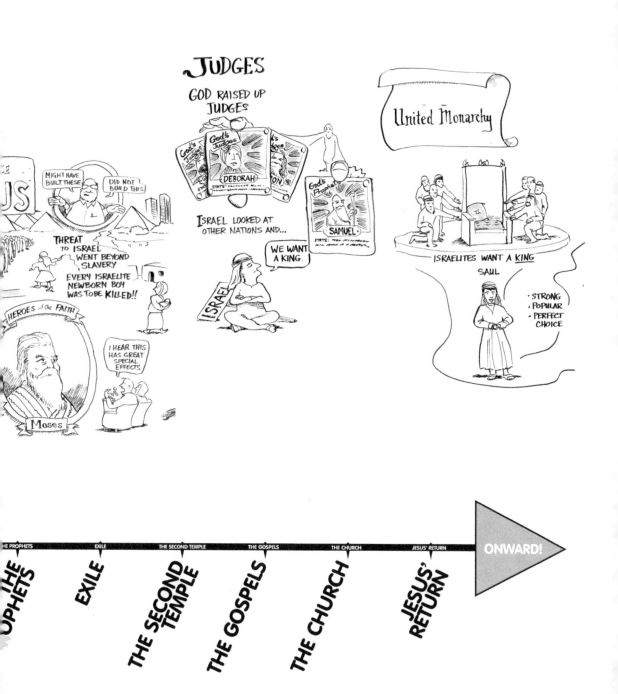

THE PROPHETS   EXILE   THE SECOND TEMPLE   THE GOSPELS   THE CHURCH   JESUS' RETURN   ONWARD!

THE PROPHETS   EXILE   THE SECOND TEMPLE   THE GOSPELS   THE CHURCH   JESUS' RETURN

DISCUSSION

Using the questions that follow, we will review and expand on the teaching we just experienced.

Let's have some fun and take a simple Bible quiz. First answer the questions as individuals, then answer them as a group. The answer key is provided in the Appendix.

THE WHITEBOARD BIBLE

1 Who covered his hands and neck with goat skins to fool his father?
    a. Ichabod
    b. Joseph
    c. Jacob
    d. Nimrod

2 Which O.T. character married a Persian king?
    a. Ruth
    b. Esther
    c. Naomi
    d. Hannah

3 Who did God send to anoint Saul as King of Israel?
    a. Moses
    b. Joshua
    c. Eli
    d. Samuel

4 Who stole her father's idols and hid them in the saddle of her camel?
    a. Leah
    b. Rachel
    c. Deborah
    d. Rebekah

5 Who killed his brother while they were in the fields?
    a. Cain
    b. Jonathon
    c. Moses
    d. Elisha

6 Who led the Israelites into the Promised Land?
    a. Moses
    b. Joseph
    c. Jesus
    d. Joshua

7 Who fled from Sodom and Gomorrah before destruction came?
    a. Gomer
    b. Saul
    c. Lot
    d. Less

8 Who was told to build an ark before a flood covered the earth?
    a. Moses
    b. Jonah
    c. Noah
    d. Abraham

9 Which king went to the witch of Endor for assistance?
    a. Hezekiah
    b. Melchizidek
    c. Solomon
    d. Saul

10 How many animals did Moses take on the ark?
    a. 2 of each kind
    b. 7 pairs of clean animals
    c. All of the above
    d. None of the above

11 Who built the Second Temple?
    a. Zerubbabel
    b. Solomon
    c. Herod
    d. David

12 Which O.T. character interpreted Nebuchadnezzar's dream?
    a. Isaiah
    b. Jeremiah
    c. Zedekiah
    d. Daniel

13 Where did Cornelius live when Peter visited his home?
    a. Smyrna
    b. Jerusalem
    c. Joppa
    d. Caesarea

14 What was Timothy's home town?
    a. Jerusalem
    b. Ephesus
    c. Lystra
    d. Phillipi

APPLICATION

Now that we've determined we all need a refresher on our Bible knowledge, let's discuss a few things we learned from Pastor Allen's lesson.

1 Have you ever read through the entire Bible?

2 How many books of the Bible can you name? (Work together on this.)

3 What is the first book of the Bible? What is the last the book of the Bible?

4 Which book of the Bible was created to help with worship?

5 Which Bible verse has been most meaningful in your life?

6 Relate a Bible story you learned in childhood and the impact it has on your life.

7 Which biblical accounts are the most difficult for you to believe?

8 How many in your group are willing to commit ten minutes a day to reading through the Bible? (At that pace, it will take about twelve months.) *See the Appendix for a daily reading plan to follow.*

PRAYER

Close the session in prayer. Share prayer requests with the group, and pray for each other. Close by praying the following prayer together.

Heavenly Father, thank You for access to Your Word. As we spend these weeks together may our hearts be open to You. Illumine our minds, quicken our memories, and grant us insight. Thank You for the opportunity to learn. Holy Spirit, we look to You as our Teacher. In Jesus' name, amen.

Prayer requests this week:

GOING DEEPER

This section is designed to do as homework, if you choose, between your Small Group meetings.

Read Psalm 1:1-6. Pastor Allen encouraged us to pursue this study with passion, realizing that God delights when His people give attention to His Word. The first psalm sets the tone for the entire collection of songs, but it also speaks to us about the expected benefits that come if we will invest the time and effort to become intimately familiar with God's Word.

- What does verse 2 tell us to meditate on and delight in?

- What does it mean to be blessed? Check out verse 3 for clues.

- What results in delighting in the law of the Lord?

- Both verse 1 and verse 6 use the idea of life as a journey. What encouragement do you gain by viewing your life as a journey?

Read Deuteronomy 17:14-20. The overview of our study brought us to the tragic and troubling time of the monarchy, when more bad than good kings led the nation. But God had long before warned His people that events would unfold exactly the way they did. Fortunately, God in His mercy always provided direction and deliverance for those who would follow.

- In verses 14-17, what typical king-like behavior were the kings of Israel specifically prohibited from doing?

- What specific instruction was given to the king regarding God's Word? How do you think this would affect leaders today if it were required of them?

DAILY REFLECTIONS

These are daily reviews of the key Bible verses and related others that will help you think about and apply the insights from this session.

DAY 1

Psalm 119:11

Uploading the Word

I have hidden your word in my heart that I might not sin against you.

Reflection Question:
How do you think *The Whiteboard Bible* study may help you in this hiding process?

DAY 2

1 Peter 2:2

Basic Nourishment

Like newborn babies, crave pure spiritual milk, so that by it you may grow up in your salvation...

Reflection Question:
In what ways can you see this study as healthy spiritual milk for your life?

DAY 3

Psalm 119:105

Illumination

Your word is a lamp to my feet and a light for my path.

Reflection Question:
What are some ways you already understand God's Word as a lamp and a light?

DAY 4

John 8:6

Finger Writing

They were using this question as a trap, in order to have a basis for accusing him. But Jesus bent down and started to write on the ground with his finger.

Reflection Question:
Any chance Jesus was the first whiteboard writer? Why was this approach such an effective way of getting a hostile audience's attention?

DAY 5

James 1:23-25

Effective Reflection

23 Anyone who listens to the word but does not do what it says is like a man who looks at his face in a mirror 24 and, after looking at himself, goes away and immediately forgets what he looks like. 25 But the man who looks intently into the perfect law that gives freedom, and continues to do this, not forgetting what he has heard, but doing it—he will be blessed in what he does.

Reflection Question:
How many times a day do you look in a mirror? Do you stop and look at God's Word a similar number of times?

WEEKLY MEMORY VERSE

JESUS ANSWERED, "IT IS WRITTEN: 'MAN DOES NOT LIVE ON BREAD ALONE, BUT ON EVERY WORD THAT COMES FROM THE MOUTH OF GOD.'"

MATTHEW 4:4

WEEK 2

INTRODUCTION

Let's start at the beginning. God chose the imagery of creation as the beginning point. From the first verse of the Bible we are invited to know God as powerful and purposeful. The reader is invited to imagine that God is concerned about people; they are unique in the midst of the wonders of creation. If we will take the step of faith to acknowledge God as Creator, the unfolding narrative of the Bible is plausible. After all, if God can create the world

CREATION

and all that is in it, what is too difficult? However, if we ignore or discount the Creation narrative the remaining pages become an increasing struggle of possibility. The Bible begins by asking us to believe there is a God and He is able to design our world. It is a very good beginning.

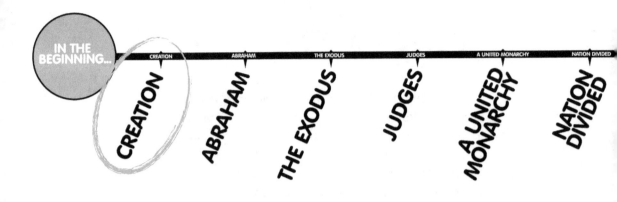

IN THE BEGINNING...

CREATION   ABRAHAM   THE EXODUS   JUDGES   A UNITED MONARCHY   NATION DIVIDED

CREATION

ABRAHAM

THE EXODUS

JUDGES

A UNITED MONARCHY

NATION DIVIDED

GETTING STARTED

Begin the session with a question below or brief activity to become better acquainted with one another.

1 What is the first thing you do when you wake up?

2 In two or three words, describe your car.

HE PROPHETS   EXILE   THE SECOND TEMPLE   THE GOSPELS   THE CHURCH   JESUS' RETURN   ONWARD!

...OPHETS

EXILE

THE SECOND TEMPLE

THE GOSPELS

THE CHURCH

JESUS' RETURN

OUTLINE OF DVD LESSON

Use the outline below to follow along during the DVD.

I. God, Our Source

II. Creation Is the Beginning

Genesis 1:1-2

¹ In the beginning God created the heavens and the earth. ² Now the earth was formless and empty, darkness was over the surface of the deep, and the Spirit of God was hovering over the waters.

A. Three Revelations in Creation

1. Image Bearers

2. Sovereignty of God

Psalm 100:3 (NASB®)

Know that the Lord Himself is God; it is He who has made us, and not we ourselves; we are His people and the sheep of His pasture.

3. Power of God and His Word

Psalm 33:6-9 (NASB®)

⁶ By the word of the Lord the heavens were made, and by the breath of His mouth all their host. ⁷ He gathers the waters of the sea together as a heap; He lays up the deeps in storehouses. ⁸ Let all the earth fear the Lord; let all the inhabitants of the world stand in awe of Him. ⁹ For He spoke, and it was done; He commanded, and it stood fast.

B. Three Lessons in Creation

1. God is all knowing (omniscient).

2. God is all powerful (omnipotent).

3. God is concerned with people.

THE WHITEBOARD BIBLE

Psalm 8:3-6

³ *When I consider your heavens, the work of your fingers, the moon and the stars, which you have set in place,* ⁴ *what is man that you are mindful of him, the son of man that you care for him?* ⁵ *You made him a little lower than the heavenly beings and crowned him with glory and honor.* ⁶ *You made him ruler over the works of your hands; you put everything under his feet...*

CREATION

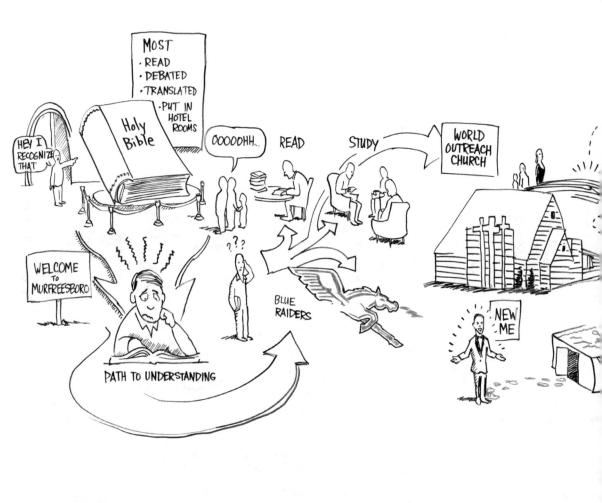

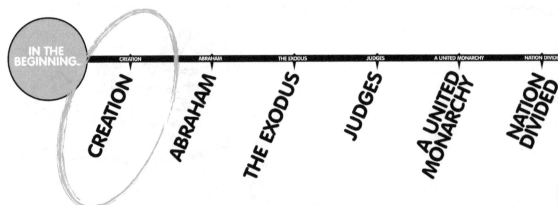

THE PROPHETS   EXILE   THE SECOND TEMPLE   THE GOSPELS   THE CHURCH   JESUS' RETURN   ONWARD!

THE PROPHETS   EXILE   THE SECOND TEMPLE   THE GOSPELS   THE CHURCH   JESUS' RETURN

DISCUSSION

Using the questions that follow, we will review and expand on the teaching we just experienced.

READ ALOUD

The Bible begins by telling us, "In the beginning God created the heavens and the earth." This is not just a poetic introduction to the Scripture—believing God as Creator is the first step necessary in understanding the rest of the Bible. Every living thing comes from God; He is our Source. The objective of the Bible is to help us understand Almighty God and His relationship with human beings on earth. He is the designer, the initiator, of all things.

1 Why do you think God started the story of the Bible by telling us about Creation?

2 Take turns reading the following passages, then answer the questions following.

Psalm 146:5-6
5 Blessed is he whose help is the God of Jacob, whose hope is in the LORD his God. 6 He is the Maker of heaven and earth, the sea, and everything in them—he remains faithful forever.

Isaiah 45:12
It is I who made the earth and created mankind upon it. My own hands stretched out the heavens; I marshaled their starry hosts.

Jeremiah 27:5
With my great power and outstretched arm I made the earth and its people and the animals that are on it, and I give it to anyone I please.

Acts 4:24 (NASB®)
And when they heard this, they lifted their voices to God with one accord and said, "O Lord, it is You who MADE THE HEAVEN AND THE EARTH AND THE SEA, AND ALL THAT IS IN THEM..."

a What is impossible for a God who is Creator? Share with the group something that you thought impossible but God proved it possible.

b What is the logical response to an Almighty Creator?

c Would there be benefits to being a friend of the Creator (such as benefits to being a friend of a celebrity, coach, authority figure, etc.)?

d Would there be consequences for being an enemy of the Creator? If so, what?

APPLICATION

Now it's time to make some personal applications of all we've been thinking about in the last few minutes.

3 God is Creator. God is sovereign, and He loves people. These aspects of God's nature are portrayed in our world. Imagine the stars and the night sky to be a declaration of God's love for you. How many stars are there? Are they randomly arranged?

4 Consider the variety of flowers, trees, and other growing things. If these represent God's concern for you, is God generous or stingy? If trees suggest something of God's love, is He understated or overstated?

5 All living creatures display God's interest for us. Imagine a variety of birds to be a declaration of God's concern for you. Do parrots, flamingos, pelicans, and hummingbirds suggest God thinks you deserve the best or leftovers?

READ ALOUD

The Bible offers no explanation for God's love for us. In spite of our rebellion, the hardness of our hearts, and our tendency to embrace ungodliness—God loves us. We matter to Him. God knows the deepest, darkest secrets of our lives and loves us anyway.

6 The beauty of the heavens and the remarkable diversity of living things reflect God's power and love for you. Our world is a remarkable demonstration of God's interest in humanity. Imagine there were no stars, our only food was oatmeal, there was only one variety of flower, and one kind of bird. What would these things suggest about God's love?

7 God had the option to design the world as He chose. God in His sovereignty made the world and everything in it for Adam and his descendants. How do you understand this message?

8 God's Word was the power used to bring order to this world. Does knowing that change the way you value time in His Word?

9 What is one idea from this session you plan to talk about with someone beyond the group this week?

PRAYER

Close the session in prayer. Share prayer requests with the group, and pray for each other. Close by praying the following prayer together.

Heavenly Father, I thank You that You are the Creator of the heavens and the earth. I am thankful that You chose to give me Your Word. I humbly ask that You would give me an understanding heart to know You. Holy Spirit, help me to know God that I might be transformed. May a love for Your Word grow within me. In Jesus' Name, amen.

Prayer requests this week:

GOING DEEPER

This section is designed to do as homework, if you choose, between your Small Group meetings.

Read Genesis 1:1-31. Understanding Creation is foundational to understanding the rest of the Bible and all of life. The Bible never makes an argument for the existence of God; it takes for granted that if we are at all aware of our status as creatures, the most obvious conclusion is that we have a Creator (Romans 1:20).

- How does each of the creative acts begin exactly the same way (vv. 3, 6, 9, 11, 14, 20, 24, 26)? How did God exercise His power?

- After the amazing creative effort of chapter 1, chapter 2 begins with a description of God at rest. What significance do you give to God's decision to not work on the seventh day?

- How does reading the creation account affect you personally?

Read Colossians 1:9–20.

- Describe in your own words the way Paul was praying for his Colossian brothers and sisters. Who would you be willing to pray for in this way?

- How do verses 13-14 relate to your own experience with Christ?

- Create a brief profile for Jesus from verses 15-20. What are His traits, strengths, and achievements? In how many ways have you directly benefitted from His work?

DAILY REFLECTIONS

These are daily reviews of the key Bible verses and related others that will help you think about and apply the insights from this session.

DAY 1

Psalm 1:1-2

A Reason to Trust God

[1] Blessed is the man who does not walk in the counsel of the wicked or stand in the way of sinners or sit in the seat of mockers. [2] But his delight is in the law of the LORD, and on his law he meditates day and night.

Reflection Question:
How are you prepared to delight in God's Word?

DAY 2

Psalm 55:22

Less Worry

Cast your cares on the LORD and he will sustain you; he will never let the righteous fall.

Reflection Question:
Make a list of worries and concerns that you can relinquish to the Lord. Remember, He will never let the righteous fall.

DAY 3

Romans 1:20

Undeniable

For since the creation of the world God's invisible qualities—his eternal power and divine nature—have been clearly seen, being understood from what has been made, so that men are without excuse.

Reflection Question:
What are some ways you remember realizing there was a God before you believed in Christ?

DAY 4

Isaiah 40:28

Tireless God

Do you not know? Have you not heard? The LORD is the everlasting God, the Creator of the ends of the earth. He will not grow tired or weary, and his understanding no one can fathom.

Reflection Question:
God never grows tired or weary. Ask God to help carry the burden for the place you are weary today.

DAY 5

Psalm 33:6-9

Reason for Awe

⁶ By the word of the LORD were the heavens made, their starry host by the breath of his mouth. ⁷ He gathers the waters of the sea into jars; he puts the deep into storehouses. Let all the earth fear the LORD; ⁸ let all the people of the world revere him. ⁹ For he spoke, and it came to be; he commanded, and it stood firm.

Reflection Question:
What part of creation inspires the greatest awe in you?

WEEKLY MEMORY VERSE

DO YOU NOT KNOW? HAVE YOU NOT HEARD? THE LORD IS THE EVERLASTING GOD, THE CREATOR OF THE ENDS OF THE EARTH. HE WILL NOT GROW TIRED OR WEARY, AND HIS UNDERSTANDING NO ONE CAN FATHOM.

ISAIAH 40:28

WEEK 3

INTRODUCTION

Welcome to week three of *The Whiteboard Bible*. Between Creation and Abraham are the universal stories of the Bible, the big picture pieces. This is where we learn about Noah and the Flood, Cain and Abel, and more. This second point of our timeline for the Bible will take us through the remainder of Genesis.

ABRAHAM

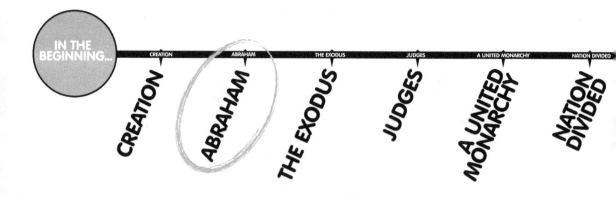

CREATION   ABRAHAM   THE EXODUS   JUDGES   A UNITED MONARCHY   NATION DIVIDED

CREATION — ABRAHAM — THE EXODUS — JUDGES — A UNITED MONARCHY — NATION DIVIDED

GETTING STARTED

44

Begin the session with a question below or brief activity to become better acquainted with one another.

1 What is your favorite story from Genesis?

2 How many have started the daily Bible reading?

THE PROPHETS   EXILE   THE SECOND TEMPLE   THE GOSPELS   THE CHURCH   JESUS' RETURN   ONWARD!

THE PROPHETS   EXILE   THE SECOND TEMPLE   THE GOSPELS   THE CHURCH   JESUS' RETURN

OUTLINE OF DVD LESSON

Use the outline below to follow along during the DVD.

I. Genesis (Beginnings)

A. Universal Themes
1. Cain and Abel
2. Noah and the Ark
3. The Tower of Babel

B. Covenant
Genesis 12:1-3

The LORD had said to Abram, "Leave your country, your people and your father's household and go to the land I will show you. ² "I will make you into a great nation and I will bless you; I will make your name great, and you will be a blessing. ³ I will bless those who bless you, and whoever curses you I will curse; and all peoples on earth will be blessed through you."

Galatians 3:14

He redeemed us in order that the blessing given to Abraham might come to the Gentiles through Christ Jesus, so that by faith we might receive the promise of the Spirit.

C. The Power of Blessing
Genesis 27:33-35

³³ Isaac trembled violently and said, "Who was it, then, that hunted game and brought it to me? I ate it just before you came and I blessed him—and indeed he will be blessed!" ³⁴ When Esau heard his father's words, he burst out with a loud and bitter cry and said to his father, "Bless me—me too, my father!" ³⁵ But he said, "Your brother came deceitfully and took your blessing."

Proverbs 18:21

The tongue has the power of life and death, and those who love it will eat its fruit.

D. Joseph In Egypt

Genesis 45:3-5

[3] *Joseph said to his brothers, "I am Joseph! Is my father still living?" But his brothers were not able to answer him, because they were terrified at his presence. [4] Then Joseph said to his brothers, "Come close to me." When they had done so, he said, "I am your brother Joseph, the one you sold into Egypt! [5] And now, do not be distressed and do not be angry with yourselves for selling me here, because it was to save lives that God sent me ahead of you."*

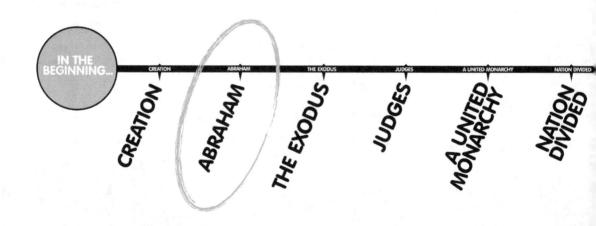

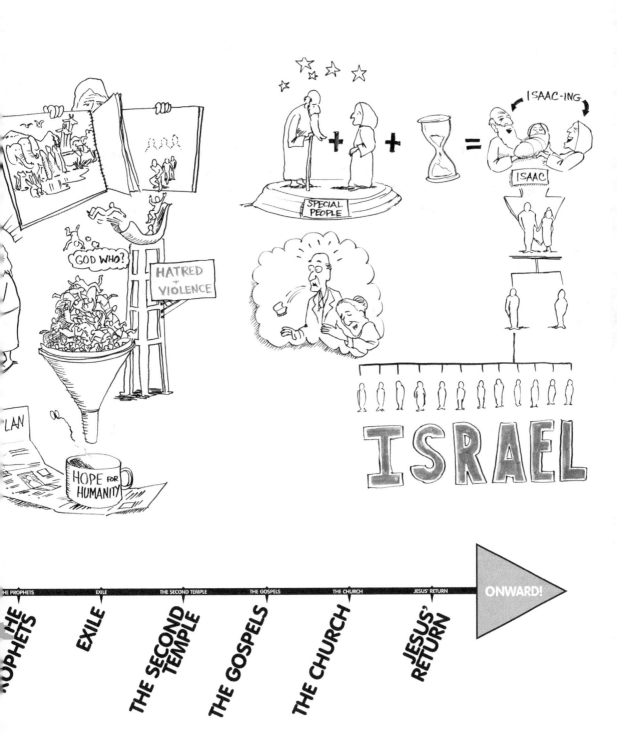

THE PROPHETS   EXILE   THE SECOND TEMPLE   THE GOSPELS   THE CHURCH   JESUS' RETURN   ONWARD!

THE PROPHETS   EXILE   THE SECOND TEMPLE   THE GOSPELS   THE CHURCH   JESUS' RETURN

DISCUSSION

Using the questions that follow, we will review and expand on the teaching we just experienced.

1   Why do you think God's primary focus of the Bible is His people?

READ ALOUD

When we get to Genesis 12, there is a shift in the story. God makes a covenant with a man named Abram. This is a pivotal point on our timeline. From Abram to the book of Revelation, God is preparing a people for Himself. The people of God are at the center of all God's activity.

2   Read Galatians 3:14. God extended the promise of Abraham to all people. How does this change your idea of being a part of God's family?

3   If God required obedience from Abraham, do you think He is interested in a response from us? Share a time when God asked you to be obedient.

APPLICATION

Now it's time to make some personal applications of all we've been thinking about in the last few minutes.

READ ALOUD

God gave a blessing to Abraham, who passed it on to his son Isaac. Isaac then had two sons, Jacob and Esau. There was tension between these brothers. In fact, we read in the Bible that God said He loved Jacob and hated Esau. Esau treated the things of God casually. For instance, when he was hungry he traded his birthright for a meal. This serves as a warning for us to not treat the things of God casually.

4 Read Genesis 27:5-40. Jacob, Esau, Rebekah, and Isaac were caught up in a struggle about inheritance. The point of debate was not land or livestock, it was "the blessing," a prayer. What did Jacob and Rebekah do to ensure Jacob would receive the blessing? How did Esau respond to their behavior?

5 Family was divided over a blessing. Jacob left with the blessing. Esau remained with the land and the livestock. The blessing seems as real as a United States Postal Service delivery. What significance do you attach to prayers of blessing or cursing? If we ignore prayer, what could we be forfeiting?

6 Discuss the differences in attitude toward God's blessing.

7 Pastor Allen reminded us that the blessing of God is tangible. What are some tangible things in life we intentionally strive to obtain? Discuss what it would look like to strive for God's blessing.

8 Read Genesis 45:3-5. Through rejection from his family, slavery in a foreign country, and wrongful imprisonment, God's purpose for Joseph was intact. Rejection, hatred, false accusations, betrayal, deprivation, and loneliness could not diminish God's purpose for Joseph. Describe a time when you've been tempted to believe God's purposes were slipping away from you?

9 Let's bundle the rejection, anger, bitterness, and our failures and ask for God's restoration so that His purpose can emerge. Take a moment this week to make a list of things you need to release into God's care.

10 Make a list of friends you think might like to join this study.

PRAYER

Close the session in prayer. Share prayer requests with the group, and pray for each other. Close by praying the following prayer together.

Heavenly Father, I rejoice that You have pronounced a blessing over my life. Thank You for creating me for a special purpose. Today, I choose God's way and to turn away from sin, unforgiveness, or anything that would hinder Your best for me. Almighty God, I ask you to restore, renew, deliver, heal—whatever is required to protect Your purpose for my life. In Jesus' name, amen.

Prayer requests this week:

GOING DEEPER

This section is designed to do as homework, if you choose, between your Small Group meetings.

Read Genesis 12:1-9; 15:1-6. Let's take a look at the call of Abraham, a man who had great faith.

- Before God's blessing would come to Abram, what did God ask him to do?

- What seven things did God say He would do for Abram?

- Who traveled with Abram?

- What was Abram's complaint to God?

- What counsel did God give to Abram?

- What promise did God make?

DAILY REFLECTIONS

These are daily reviews of the key Bible verses and related others that will help you think about and apply the insights from this session.

THE **WHITEBOARD** BIBLE

DAY 1

Genesis 12:1-3

When God Calls

¹ The LORD had said to Abram, "Leave your country, your people and your father's household and go to the land I will show you. ² I will make you into a great nation and I will bless you; I will make your name great, and you will be a blessing. ³ I will bless those who bless you, and whoever curses you I will curse; and all peoples on earth will be blessed through you."

Reflection Question:
What are the blessings given to Abraham for obeying the Word of God?

DAY 2

Galatians 3:14

Priceless Inheritance

He redeemed us in order that the blessing given to Abraham might come to the Gentiles through Christ Jesus, so that by faith we might receive the promise of the Spirit.

Reflection Question:
How would you describe your own experience of God's promise to you?

DAY 3

Genesis 22:6-8

God's Faithfulness

⁶ Abraham took the wood for the burnt offering and placed it on his son Isaac, and he himself carried the fire and the knife. As the two of them went on together, ⁷ Isaac spoke up and said to his father Abraham, "Father?" "Yes, my son?" Abraham replied. "The fire and wood are here," Isaac said, "but where is the lamb for the burnt offering?" ⁸ Abraham answered, "God himself will provide the lamb for the burnt offering, my son." And the two of them went on together.

Reflection Question:
Who have you told recently about the evidences of God's faithfulness in your life? What examples did you use?

DAY 4

Genesis 45:4-5

How God Works

4 Then Joseph said to his brothers, "Come close to me." When they had done so, he said, "I am your brother Joseph, the one you sold into Egypt! 5 And now, do not be distressed and do not be angry with yourselves for selling me here, because it was to save lives that God sent me ahead of you."

Reflection Question:
What circumstances in your life have prepared you for where you are today?

DAY 5

Romans 8:28

God's Hand in All Things

And we know that in all things God works for the good of those who love him, who have been called according to his purpose.

Reflection Question:
In what ways can you see this amazing truth from the New Testament illustrated in the life of Joseph?

WEEKLY MEMORY VERSE

AND WE KNOW THAT IN ALL THINGS GOD WORKS FOR THE GOOD OF THOSE WHO LOVE HIM, WHO HAVE BEEN CALLED ACCORDING TO HIS PURPOSE.

ROMANS 8:28

WEEK 4

INTRODUCTION

This week we will consider God's powerful deliverance of the Hebrew people from Egyptian slavery. The Exodus is the greatest example of God's deliverance until we see Jesus' redemptive work. Genesis concludes with a family moving to Egypt. When the book of Exodus opens, hundreds of years have passed and the family has grown into a multitude of people. God's compassion and power are on display as He steps into the midst of history to watch over

THE EXODUS

His purposes. God still watches over our lives; the lessons of Exodus are relevant for us.

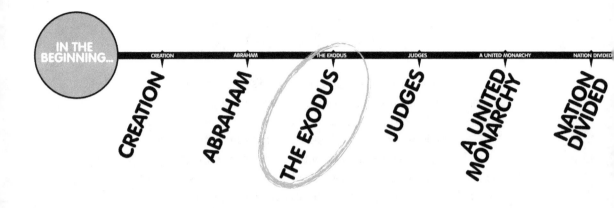

IN THE BEGINNING...

CREATION · ABRAHAM · THE EXODUS · JUDGES · A UNITED MONARCHY · NATION DIVIDED

CREATION ABRAHAM THE EXODUS JUDGES A UNITED MONARCHY NATION DIVIDED

GETTING STARTED

Begin the session with a question below or brief activity to become better acquainted with one another.

1 What is the most memorable camping trip you have ever taken?

2 How is this study helping you to better understand the Bible?

THE PROPHETS   EXILE   THE SECOND TEMPLE   THE GOSPELS   THE CHURCH   JESUS' RETURN   ONWARD!

THE PROPHETS

EXILE

THE SECOND TEMPLE

THE GOSPELS

THE CHURCH

JESUS' RETURN

OUTLINE OF DVD LESSON
Use the outline below to follow along during the DVD.

I. Deliverance

Exodus 3:6-8

6 Then he said, "I am the God of your father, the God of Abraham, the God of Isaac and the God of Jacob." At this, Moses hid his face, because he was afraid to look at God. 7 The LORD said, "I have indeed seen the misery of my people in Egypt. I have heard them crying out because of their slave drivers, and I am concerned about their suffering. 8 So I have come down to rescue them from the hand of the Egyptians and to bring them up out of that land into a good and spacious land, a land flowing with milk and honey—the home of the Canaanites, Hittites, Amorites, Perizzites, Hivites and Jebusites."

A. Wilderness

Exodus 13:17-18, 21-22

17 When Pharaoh let the people go, God did not lead them on the road through the Philistine country, though that was shorter. For God said, "If they face war, they might change their minds and return to Egypt." 18 So God led the people around by the desert road toward the Red Sea. . . . 21 By day the LORD went ahead of them in a pillar of cloud to guide them on their way and by night in a pillar of fire to give them light, so that they could travel by day or night. 22 Neither the pillar of cloud by day nor the pillar of fire by night left its place in front of the people.

B. Marah

Exodus 15:23-24

23 When they came to Marah, they could not drink its water because it was bitter . . . 24 So the people grumbled against Moses, saying, "What are we to drink?"

C. Manna

Exodus 16:2-5

*2 In the desert the whole community grumbled against Moses and Aaron.
3 The Israelites said to them, "If only we had died by the Lord's hand in
Egypt! There we sat around pots of meat and ate all the food we wanted,
but you have brought us out into this desert to starve this entire assembly to
death." 4 Then the Lord said to Moses, "I will rain down bread from heaven
for you. The people are to go out each day and gather enough for that day.
In this way I will test them and see whether they will follow my instructions.
5 On the sixth day they are to prepare what they bring in, and that is to be
twice as much as they gather on the other days."*

D. Grumbling

E. Ten Commandments

F. The Tabernacle

G. Refusal to Trust

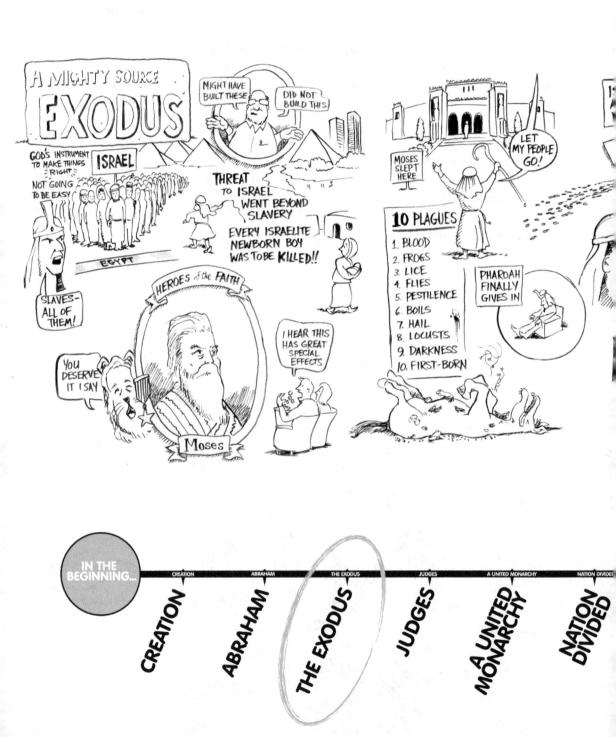

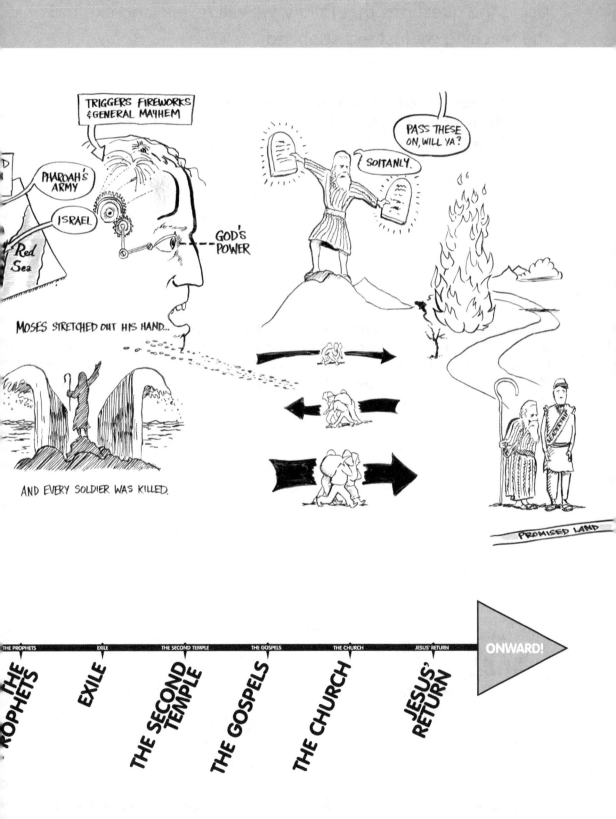

DISCUSSION

Using the questions that follow, we will review and expand on the teaching we just experienced.

1 Describe a favorite scene from the movie *The Ten Commandments*. Does the movie make the biblical narrative more believable or more like a fantasy?

2 Exodus is the account of the Israelites leaving where? Who was the leader that God provided as a catalyst for the events of Exodus?

READ ALOUD
For forty years Moses had been living in the desert because of a moment of rage. Then he had an encounter at the burning bush, and God handed him an assignment. God is in the business of restoring people. Almost every character we look at in Scripture has a season when God lifts them above their own failures. God is a redeeming God.

3 List a few of the ways God involved Himself in the lives of the Israelites. Do you imagine God is still involved in the direction of people and nations? How?

4 In Exodus God is a deliverer, provider, and protector. From your life experience describe events when God has delivered, provided, and protected.

APPLICATION

Now it's time to make some personal applications of all
we've been thinking about in the last few minutes.

Being Set Free:

The Components
- God revealed as Deliverer
- Moses, a reluctant leader
- Pharaoh, a stubborn antagonist
- Plagues, God's power on display
- Freedom, a new beginning for God's people

5 Read Exodus 3:7-10.

a. God said He had seen, heard, and was concerned about His people.
What was God concerned about?

b. God's response to His people involves two things:
1) to rescue them and
2) _____.

READ ALOUD

**Before God recruited Moses to confront Pharaoh, Moses had murdered an
Egyptian and was forced to flee into the desert. God uses flawed people—
there is no other kind. God's power transforms our flaws and failures into
useful parts of our character.**

6 Read Exodus 2:11-12. Can you recognize one of your flaws or failures that
God has transformed into a strength? Explain.

Lessons in Freedom:

The Components
- Better to be God's people
- Free but still dependent upon God
- God's love expressed in boundaries
- Delivered for a specific destination

7 As the Israelites moved away from the Red Sea, they were free and Egypt was in total disarray. It is better to be God's people. From your experience describe benefits and challenges of being "God's people."

8 The Israelites were free of Egypt but still needed God's help for daily provision. Why do circumstances that require dependence on God often feel so unpleasant?

9 Freedom is not independence from God; it is a confident assurance God is present for whatever challenges occur. Where would you like to experience greater freedom?

10 God provided guidance for the Israelites in the form of rules and regulations–life's warning labels. God's love would not be complete if He did not warn us about destructive outcomes. Is accepting boundaries easy or difficult for you? Describe a circumstance when you benefitted from a rule or boundary.

11 God sets us free for a purpose, and without His direction we will enslave ourselves again. Describe ways you are learning to cooperate with God's purposes. Can you identify freedoms associated with your obedience?

Freedom Challenges:

The Components
- Bitter places
- Wrong responses
- Expressions of grace

12 God led the Israelites to a place where the water was bitter; He had a plan. Take a step of faith and thank God for the bitter places you have walked through.

13 Grumbling is normal but not helpful. Grumbling is about our heart more than our circumstances. Thankfulness is the antidote for grumbling. Ingratitude is the catalyst for complaining. Take a moment and list four or five things for which you can express gratitude. Share your list with the group. Discuss ways to maintain a thankful/appreciative attitude this week.

READ ALOUD

Exodus is an account of a journey. You are living out a God-journey. The names are changed, but many of the components are similar: dreams, failures, antagonists, fear, God's involvement, confusion, and the challenges of learning. God has a plan for your good!

PRAYER

Close the session in prayer. Share prayer requests with the group, and pray for each other. Close by praying the following prayer together.

Heavenly Father, thank You for caring for me. I know Your grace and mercy surround me. Today I turn my face to You asking for Your help. May Your power bring freedom and deliverance to my life. I choose to cooperate with You, to yield to Your instruction. Forgive my grumbling. May a spirit of thanksgiving grow within me. May my life be pleasing in Your sight. Grant me a spirit of contentment as I follow Your path. In Jesus' name, amen.

Prayer requests this week:

GOING DEEPER

This section is designed to do as homework, if you choose, between your Small Group meetings.

Read Exodus 20:1-17.

- List the Ten Commandments.

- How many of them are prohibitive?

- How many of them are directive?

- Which commandments come with a promise?

- The Ten Commandments were a part of God's provision for His people. Why do you suppose there is so much controversy surrounding these principles for life?

- Do these commandments seem like they would help or hinder contemporary society?

THE **WHITEBOARD** BIBLE

DAILY REFLECTIONS

These are daily reviews of the key Bible verses and related others that will help you think about and apply the insights from this session.

DAY 1

Deuteronomy 6:4-6
Doorframes

4 Hear, O Israel: The LORD our God, the LORD is one. 5 Love the LORD your God with all your heart and with all your soul and with all your strength. 6 These commandments that I give you today are to be on your hearts.

Reflection Question:
How are we to love the Lord?

DAY 2

Exodus 15:2
Strength

"The LORD is my strength and my song; he has become my salvation. He is my God, and I will praise him, my father's God, and I will exalt him."

Reflection Question:
We gain strength when we exalt God. What things can you praise Him for today?

DAY 3

Exodus 3:6-8
When God Moves

7 The LORD said, "I have indeed seen the misery of my people in Egypt. I have heard them crying out because of their slave drivers, and I am concerned about their suffering. 8 So I have come down to rescue them from the hand of the Egyptians and to bring them up out of that land into a good and spacious land, a land flowing with milk and honey—the home of the Canaanites, Hittites, Amorites, Perizzites, Hivites and Jebusites."

Reflection Question:
Over what matters in your life would you say you have really "cried out" to God? What has been the result of seeking and waiting for His answers?

DAY 4

God's Purpose

"But I have raised you up for this very purpose, that I might show you my power and that my name might be proclaimed in all the earth."

Reflection Question:
This cannot have been good news that Moses delivered to Pharaoh. What two purposes are behind all God does? In what ways is God still accomplishing these purposes in your life?

DAY 5

Exodus 13:21-22

God's Way

21 By day the LORD went ahead of them in a pillar of cloud to guide them on their way and by night in a pillar of fire to give them light, so that they could travel by day or night. 22 Neither the pillar of cloud by day nor the pillar of fire by night left its place in front of the people.

Reflection Question:
How did the Lord lead them? How is He leading you?

WEEKLY MEMORY VERSE

"THE LORD IS MY STRENGTH AND MY SONG; HE HAS BECOME MY SALVATION. HE IS MY GOD, AND I WILL PRAISE HIM, MY FATHER'S GOD, AND I WILL EXALT HIM."

EXODUS 15:2

WEEK 5

INTRODUCTION

By now we should be settling into a level of comfort with the group while continuing to welcome any newcomers. In this session we will consider the people of Israel as they complete their time in the wilderness and begin to occupy the Promised Land. Surprisingly the transition is frightening, awkward, and even confrontational. Often we mistakenly equate following God with easy and simple. As we process the Israelites'

JUDGES

journey, we will reflect on our own. We each want God's best. We must allow faith and obedience to triumph over fear and other obstacles.

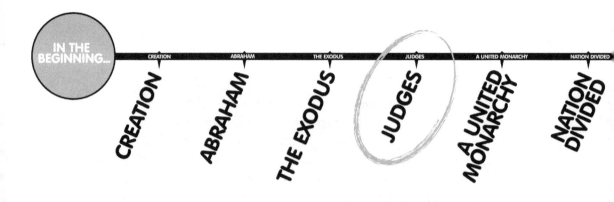

IN THE BEGINNING...

CREATION   ABRAHAM   THE EXODUS   JUDGES   A UNITED MONARCHY   NATION DIVIDED

CREATION

ABRAHAM

THE EXODUS

JUDGES

A UNITED MONARCHY

NATION DIVIDED

GETTING STARTED

Begin the session with a question below or brief activity to become better acquainted with one another.

1 Share with the group one of your greatest accomplishments you couldn't have done without God's help.

2 Spend a few minutes reviewing the key points we have covered so far in this study.

THE PROPHETS
EXILE
THE SECOND TEMPLE
THE GOSPELS
THE CHURCH
JESUS' RETURN

81

OUTLINE OF DVD LESSON

Use the outline below to follow along during the DVD.

I. Joshua

Joshua 1:6-7

[6] *"Be strong and courageous, because you will lead these people to inherit the land I swore to their forefathers to give them. [7] Be strong and very courageous..."*

Acts 4:13

When they saw the courage of Peter and John and realized that they were unschooled, ordinary men, they were astonished and they took note that these men had been with Jesus.

Philippians 4:13

I can do everything through him who gives me strength.

II. Judges

A. Cycle of Retribution

B. Gideon

Judges 6:11-12

[11] *The angel of the Lord came and sat down under the oak in Ophrah that belonged to Joash the Abiezrite, where his son Gideon was threshing wheat in a winepress to keep it from the Midianites. [12] When the angel of the Lord appeared to Gideon, he said, "The Lord is with you, mighty warrior."*

1. Questions about circumstances
2. Inadequate resources and experience

Judges 6:27

27 So Gideon took ten of his servants and did as the LORD told him. But because he was afraid of his family and the men of the town, he did it at night rather than in the daytime.

1. Addressed personal challenges
2. Followed God while afraid

Judges 7:2

The LORD said to Gideon, "You have too many men. I cannot deliver Midian into their hands, or Israel would boast against me, 'My own strength has saved me.'"

1. Too many resources
2. Pride and self-sufficiency

JUDGES

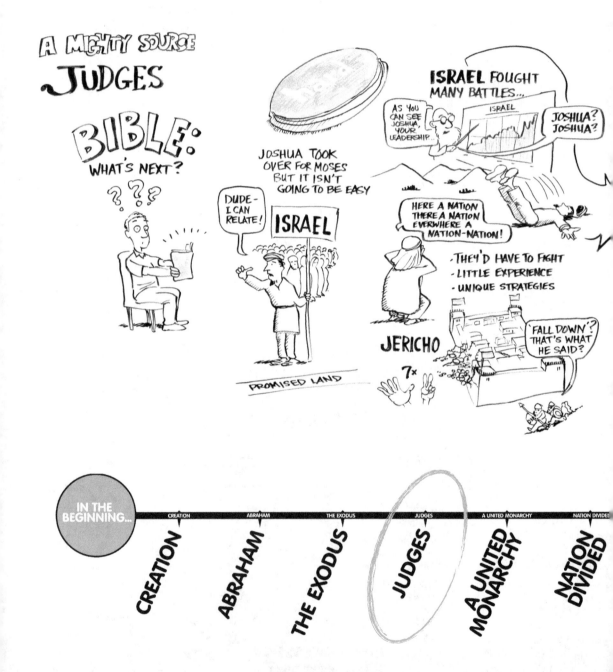

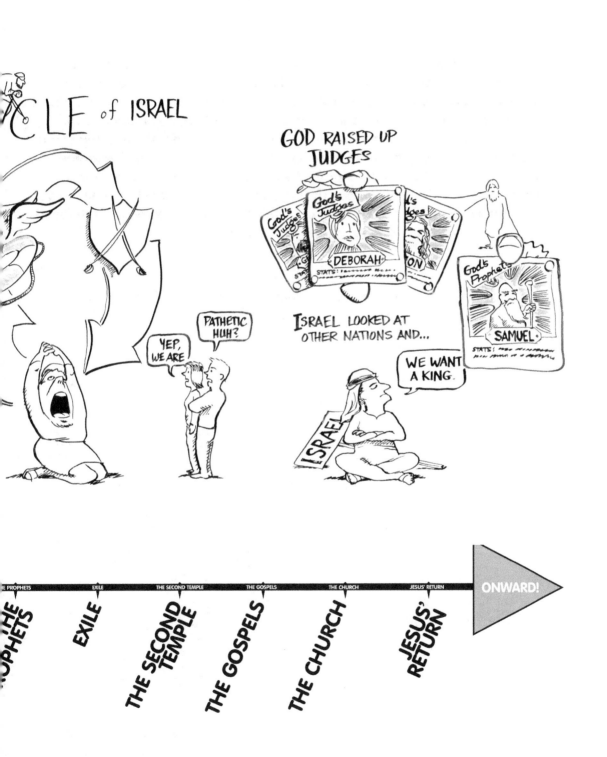

DISCUSSION

Using the questions that follow, we will review and expand on the teaching we just experienced.

READ ALOUD

Joshua was Moses' successor. He was given the assignment to complete what Moses couldn't complete. God told Joshua seven times to "be strong and very courageous." If God told him seven times, what do we know about Joshua? He was frightened and discouraged. The task was intimidating, but Joshua was faithful and did what God told him to do. Even though God said the land belonged to the Israelites, they had to secure it. Sometimes we imagine that the promises of God will come to us without resistance, without conflict. If we use the scripture as our pattern, we should not expect the journey to be easy. The most remarkable men and women of faith faced conflict in receiving and fulfilling the promises of God.

1 Joshua was Moses' successor. What event from Moses' life is most remarkable to you?

2 What feelings did you have when someone who was a great strength in your life died?

3 God provided leaders for His people: Moses, Joshua, Gideon, etc. Which leaders have influenced your life? In what ways?

4 Each of us has a sphere of influence. Are you conscious of leading/influencing others? Identify ways you influence other people to honor God.

GOD RAISED UP JUDGES

God's Judges

God's Judges

•DEBORAH•

STATS:

ISRAEL LOOKED AT OTHER NATIONS AND..

APPLICATION

Now it's time to make some personal applications of all we've been thinking about in the last few minutes.

5 Read Joshua 1:1-9. What was God's commandment (not suggestion) to Joshua?

a Joshua apparently was frightened and discouraged by the prospect of leading the Israelites in Moses' absence. Has the prospect of following God ever been frightening to you? What was the outcome when you responded?

b Joshua had been in training for forty years. He was still anxious. God told him to give attention to His instructions "day and night" (v. 8). How do you maintain a focus on God's direction for your life? What is the most effective help when you are discouraged?

c How did the Israelites occupy the Promised Land, through conflict or by a parade? What are the implications for our own spiritual journey? Read Ephesians 6:10-12. What spiritual struggles have you faced in recent months? What role have strength and courage played in your victory?

THE **WHITEBOARD** BIBLE

READ ALOUD

In Judges 6:12 God called Gideon a "mighty warrior" even when he was filled with fear and in hiding. God invited Gideon to serve, knowing Gideon was frightened. He also invites us to follow and serve when we feel unprepared.

6 Read Judges 6:11-16. Relate a time you were willing to serve God even though you felt inadequate.

7 God sees in you the potential to make a difference, just like He did in Gideon. What places of influence or authority are present in your life? How can you share your Jesus-story in those places?

8 The book of Judges reminds us that every generation needs a voice for God. Discuss ways you can be a "voice" for the Kingdom of God more effectively.

9 Read Ephesians 2:10. God is still writing His story in the earth. We are the latest edition. After four weeks together your group has begun a new journey—take a moment and share the ways you see God's workmanship in one another.

10 A person of faith makes a difference. Describe when someone with faith made a difference in your life.

PRAYER

Close the session in prayer. Share prayer requests with the group, and pray for each other. Before we conclude, we want to ask God to use our lives for His purposes. God will help us to overcome our fears and inadequacies. In our weakness, He is glorified.

Heavenly Father, thank You for choosing me. You called me out of darkness and welcomed me into the Kingdom of Your Son. I rejoice today that I belong to the Kingdom of God. Open my ears to listen and my heart to respond to Your invitations. Forgive me for my stubbornness and reluctance to cooperate. Give me wisdom to honor You with my days, to utilize the gifts and opportunities entrusted to me. May my life bring glory and honor to my Lord. In Jesus' name, amen.

Prayer requests this week:

GOING DEEPER

This section is designed to do as homework, if you choose, between your Small Group meetings.

Read Judges 13:1-5; 14:19-20; 16:20-31.

- Before God chose Samson, He chose his parents. What were their names?

- What requirements were listed that would qualify Samson as a Nazarite?

- Why was Jesus called a Nazarene? Read Matthew 2:22-23.

- What is the key to Samson's strength?

- How did the Philistines subdue Samson?

- What did they do with Samson after he was captured?

- How did Samson end his life, in triumph or tragedy?

...RAEL LOOKED AT OTHER NATIONS AND...

WE WANT A KING.

ISRAEL

DAILY REFLECTIONS

These are daily reviews of the key Bible verses and related others that will help you think about and apply the insights from this session.

DAY 1

Joshua 24:15

Making Your Stand

"But if serving the LORD seems undesirable to you, then choose for yourselves this day whom you will serve, whether the gods your forefathers served beyond the River, or the gods of the Amorites, in whose land you are living. But as for me and my household, we will serve the LORD."

Reflection Question:

To what degree and in what ways have you and your family taken a stand for God as Joshua did in his day?

DAY 2

Joshua 1:8-9

The Mighty Source

8 "Do not let this Book of the Law depart from your mouth; meditate on it day and night, so that you may be careful to do everything written in it. Then you will be prosperous and successful. 9 Have I not commanded you? Be strong and courageous. Do not be terrified; do not be discouraged, for the LORD your God will be with you wherever you go."

Reflection Question:

What did God mean by telling Joshua not to let His Word "depart from your mouth"? How are the two verses parallel in meaning?

DAY 3

Judges 2:10

Legacy

After that whole generation had been gathered to their fathers, another generation grew up, who knew neither the LORD nor what he had done for Israel.

Reflection Question:

How are you taking steps to make sure the generation that follows you knows God and what He has done for you in your lifetime?

DAY 4

Judges 8:23

Declining an Offer

But Gideon told them,
"I will not rule over you,
nor will my son rule over
you. The LORD will rule
over you."

Reflection Question:
What are some ways
we can remember not
to place ourselves or
let others place us in
positions where we try
to do what only God
can do?

DAY 5

Judges 6:27

Overcoming Fears

So Gideon took ten of
his servants and did as
the LORD told him. But
because he was afraid of
his family and the men of
the town, he did it at night
rather than in the daytime.

Reflection Question:
What things do you fear
that cause you to be
reluctant to follow God?

WEEKLY MEMORY VERSE

8 "Do not let this
Book of the Law
depart from your
mouth; meditate on
it day and night,
so that you may
be careful to do
everything written
in it. Then you will
be prosperous and
successful. 9 Have
I not commanded
you? Be strong and
courageous. Do not
be terrified; do not
be discouraged, for
the Lord your God
will be with you
wherever you go."

Joshua 1:8-9

WEEK 6

INTRODUCTION

In this session we will explore the transition between the independent tribes of Israel and the first kings: Saul, David, and Solomon. God's people once again are struggling with the challenges of change and understanding how to honor God. The gravitational pull away from God is not new to the twenty-first century; it has plagued people since antiquity. God's grace made a way forward for the ancient Israelites, just as it will for you and me.

UNITED MONARCHY

ISRAELITES WANT A KING

SAUL

- STRONG
- POPULAR
- PERFECT CHOICE

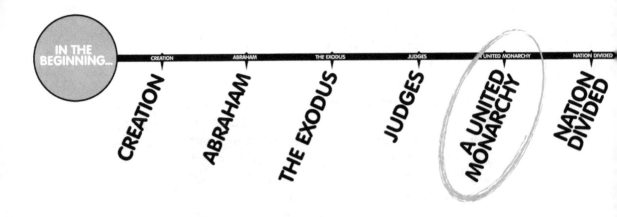

GETTING STARTED

Begin the session with a question below or brief activity to become better acquainted with one another.

1 If you could be a king for a day, what would you request?

2 Have you ever visited a castle? Describe your experience.

THE PROPHETS   EXILE   THE SECOND TEMPLE   THE GOSPELS   THE CHURCH   JESUS' RETURN   ONWARD!

THE PROPHETS
EXILE
THE SECOND TEMPLE
THE GOSPELS
THE CHURCH
JESUS' RETURN

99

OUTLINE OF DVD LESSON

Use the outline below to follow along during the DVD.

I. The Monarchy

A. Samuel

1 Samuel 8:7, 9

7 And the LORD told him: "Listen to all that the people are saying to you; it is not you they have rejected, but they have rejected me as their king... 9 Now listen to them; but warn them solemnly and let them know what the king who will reign over them will do."

1 Samuel 8:19-22

19 But the people refused to listen to Samuel. "No!" they said. "We want a king over us. 20 Then we will be like all the other nations, with a king to lead us and to go out before us and fight our battles." 21 When Samuel heard all that the people said, he repeated it before the LORD. 22 The LORD answered, "Listen to them and give them a king." Then Samuel said to the men of Israel, "Everyone go back to his town."

B. Saul

1 Samuel 9:1-2; 10:1

1 There was a Benjamite, a man of standing, whose name was Kish... 2 He had a son named Saul, an impressive young man without equal among the Israelites—a head taller than any of the others.

1 Then Samuel took a flask of oil and poured it on Saul's head and kissed him, saying, "Has not the LORD anointed you leader over his inheritance?"

C. David

1 Samuel 16:11-13

11 So he asked Jesse, "Are these all the sons you have?" "There is still the youngest," Jesse answered, "but he is tending the sheep." Samuel said, "Send for him; we will not sit down until he arrives."12 So he sent for him and had him brought in. He was ruddy, with a fine appearance and handsome features. Then the LORD said, "Rise and anoint him; he is the one."

¹³ *So Samuel took the horn of oil and anointed him in the presence of his brothers, and from that day on the Spirit of the Lord came upon David in power. Samuel then went to Ramah.*

D. Solomon
2 Chronicles 1:11-12

¹¹ *God said to Solomon, "Since this is your heart's desire and you have not asked for wealth, riches or honor, nor for the death of your enemies, and since you have not asked for a long life but for wisdom and knowledge to govern my people over whom I have made you king,* ¹² *therefore wisdom and knowledge will be given you. And I will also give you wealth, riches and honor, such as no king who was before you ever had and none after you will have."*

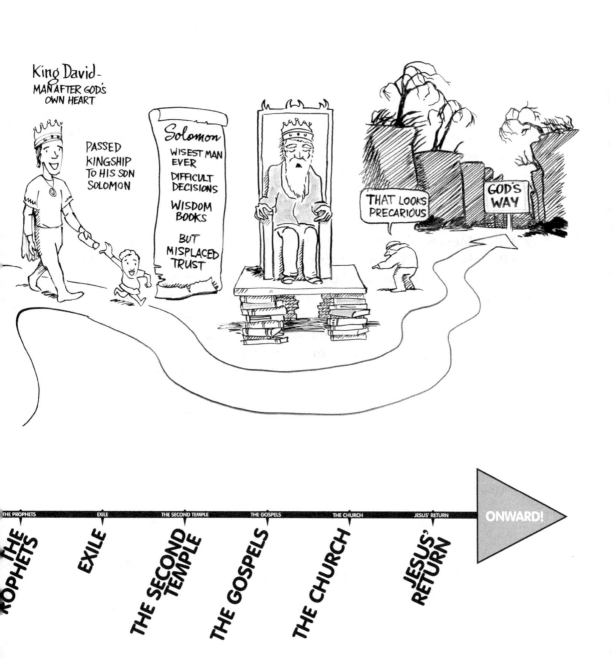

THE PROPHETS   EXILE   THE SECOND TEMPLE   THE GOSPELS   THE CHURCH   JESUS' RETURN   ONWARD!

THE PROPHETS   EXILE   THE SECOND TEMPLE   THE GOSPELS   THE CHURCH   JESUS' RETURN

DISCUSSION

Using the questions that follow, we will review and expand on the teaching we just experienced.

1   Can you name the first five books of the Bible from memory?

2   What is your favorite Old Testament/Hebrew Bible story?

3   Leviticus, Numbers, and Deuteronomy all emerge from the years in the wilderness, between Egypt and the Promised Land. Who was the leader of God's people during this time?

READ ALOUD

The United Monarchy was a pivotal point for the Israelites. They had been in the Promised Land for hundreds of years. Their form of government was a theocracy in which God ruled over them through a series of judges. The last of the judges was Samuel. The leaders of the tribes told Samuel they did not want him to rule over them anymore—they wanted to be like all the other nations. They wanted a king. Samuel told the people what a king would do for them, but they would not listen. It is a lesson for us—we must learn to listen for God's perspective in our lives. Throughout Scripture, one of the most consistent characteristics of the people of God is that they listen to Him.

King David—
MAN AFTER GOD'S OWN HEART

PASSED KINGSHIP TO HIS SON SOLOMON

4   Who were the first three kings of Israel?

5   David and Solomon, though father and son, were very different men. What factors contributed to these differences?

APPLICATION

Now it's time to make some personal applications of all we've been thinking about in the last few minutes.

1 Read 1 Samuel 8:4-5. Describe a time when God's blessings came to your life even though you were not cooperating fully with Him.

2 Read 1 Samuel 8:19-22. In verse 19 the people refused to_____.

a In verse 22 the Lord instructs Samuel to _____.

b Listening requires us to focus our attention on someone else, ignore distractions, and focus on their thoughts. How do you listen to God? Have you ever ignored God? Have you ever intentionally cooperated with God?

c Discuss ways you can improve your "spiritual listening skills."

THAT
PRECA

3   Read Acts 13:22. David's greatest asset was his willingness to cooperate with God. Identify one way you can cooperate with God more completely.

a   David had great strengths and weaknesses. List some of his victories/accomplishments and some of his failures.

4   Read 2 Chronicles 1:8-12. Solomon is noted for his wisdom. It was a gift/ability from God—not the result of study or training. What gifts has God entrusted to you?

a   Solomon built the first Temple in Jerusalem. It was a tremendous honor given to him by God. The Temple was built on Mt Moriah. Who offered the first sacrifice on Mt. Moriah?

b   Saul, David, and Solomon all had opportunities to serve God, in spite of their flaws and failures. So do we. Take a moment and discuss ways you can honor God from the position He has given you.

5   As a group make plans now to work through Volume 2 of *The Whiteboard Bible*. You can learn the story of the Bible with just a little effort. You are off to a good start, so don't lose your momentum. Keep reading!

PRAYER

Close the session in prayer. Share prayer requests with the group, and pray for each other. Close by praying the following prayer together.

Heavenly Father, thank You for sending Jesus into the earth. Your care and provision for my life is elaborate. Awaken my ears to listen and my heart to receive. I choose to cooperate with You, to yield to Your direction, and daily submit my will to Yours. Give me strength to complete the course You have created me for. I rejoice in my Lord and Redeemer. Amen.

Prayer requests this week:

GOING DEEPER

This section is designed to do as homework, if you choose, between your Small Group meetings.

Read 1 Samuel 16:1-13. The encounter between Samuel and David is noteworthy in several ways. God told him what family to approach but not which son. Samuel had been impressed by Saul's appearance, and he was about to learn a lesson about God's way of choosing people to serve Him. The task David was occupied with fit into the category of chores no one else wanted. Clearly the seven older brothers had insisted that David should be the shepherd in the family. Little did they know God was using his banishment to expose David to the skills he would require later as God's man on the throne.

- In verse 7 God responds to Samuel's assumption that the handsome oldest brother must God's chosen: *But the LORD said to Samuel, "Do not consider his appearance or his height, for I have rejected him. The LORD does not look at the things man looks at. Man looks at the outward appearance, but the LORD looks at the heart."* What is God looking for in a man's heart?

- What is your impression of the young man David who was presented to Samuel in verse 12?

- As you think about God's participation in this event, what lessons do you think He wanted us to take from the anointing of David as the new king?

Read 1 Samuel 17:1-58. The faceoff between David and Goliath has long been a prime example of the role of the underdog. When someone is obviously expected to lose a contest, they often resort to creative thinking that never crosses the mind of the superior opponent who is anticipating victory. Presumably Goliath had faced and crushed many fighting men who met him under conditions that suited his superior size and strength. David may have been the first opponent to face him who ignored those limitations. As many have noted, to others, Goliath was too great an enemy to defeat; to David, Goliath was too big a target to miss. The very things that seemed to make Goliath invincible made him shockingly vulnerable in an encounter with a fighter like David.

- What is David's initial response to Goliath's taunts? What could have been the cause for Eliab, David's oldest brother, to respond the way he did?

- When questioned by Saul, what resumé does David offer as qualifications to face Goliath?

- Verses 41-49 record the actual encounter between Goliath and David. How many points of difference can you find in the comments made by each opponent toward the other?

- What was David's mighty source? How did his strength and courage influence those around him?

DAILY REFLECTIONS

These are daily reviews of the key Bible verses and related others that will help you think about and apply the insights from this session.

DAY 1

1 Samuel 8:7-9

Rejections

⁷ *And the LORD told him: "Listen to all that the people are saying to you; it is not you they have rejected, but they have rejected me as their king.* ⁸ *As they have done from the day I brought them up out of Egypt until this day, forsaking me and serving other gods, so they are doing to you.* ⁹ *Now listen to them; but warn them solemnly and let them know what the king who will reign over them will do."*

Reflection Question:
What are some of the danger signs that warn us when we are doing the same thing toward God that the Israelites did?

DAY 2

Psalm 23:1-3

Our Shepherd

¹ *The LORD is my shepherd, I shall not be in want.* ² *He makes me lie down in green pastures, he leads me beside quiet waters,* ³ *he restores my soul. He guides me in paths of righteousness for his name's sake.*

Reflection Question:
God's shepherding role also has king-like qualities. How do you experience those in your life?

DAY 3

1 Samuel 16:7

God's Perspective

But the LORD said to Samuel, "Do not consider his appearance or his height, for I have rejected him. The LORD does not look at the things man looks at. Man looks at the outward appearance, but the LORD looks at the heart."

Reflection Question:
Which part of us draws God's attention? Which part of us do we invest the most effort in?

DAY 4

Acts 13:22

Determined Obedience

"After removing Saul, he made David their king. He testified concerning him: 'I have found David son of Jesse a man after my own heart; he will do everything I want him to do.'"

Reflection Question:
What does God commend David for? Where are you most reluctant to cooperate with God?

DAY 5

Proverbs 3:5-6

Wisdom Ignored

5 Trust in the LORD with all your heart and lean not on your own understanding; 6 in all your ways acknowledge him, and he will make your paths straight.

Reflection Question:
What is the connection between your heart condition and your understanding?

WEEKLY MEMORY VERSE

5 TRUST IN THE LORD WITH ALL YOUR HEART AND LEAN NOT ON YOUR OWN UNDERSTANDING; 6 IN ALL YOUR WAYS ACKNOWLEDGE HIM, AND HE WILL MAKE YOUR PATHS STRAIGHT.

PROVERBS 3:5-6

APPENDIX

FREQUENTLY ASKED QUESTIONS

What do we do on the first night of our group?
Like all fun things in life–have a party! A "get to know you" coffee, dinner, or dessert is a great way to launch a new study. You may want to review the Group Agreement page and share the names of a few friends you can invite to join you. But most important, have fun before your study time begins.

Where do we find new members for our group?
We encourage you to pray with your group and then brainstorm a list of people from work, church, your neighborhood, your children's school, family, the gym, and so forth. Then have each group member invite several of the people on his or her list.

No matter how you find participants, it's vital that you stay on the lookout for new people to join your group. All groups tend to go through healthy attrition–the result of moves, releasing new leaders, ministry opportunities, and so forth–and if the group gets too small, it could be at risk of shutting down. If you and your group stay open, you'll be amazed at the people God sends your way. The next person just might become a friend for life. You never know!

How long will this group meet?
It's totally up to the group–once you come to the end of this six-week study. Most groups meet weekly for at least their first six weeks, but every other week can work as well.

At the end of this study, each group member may decide if he or she wants to continue on for another six-week study. Some groups launch relationships for years to come, and others are stepping-stones into another group experience. Either way, enjoy the journey.

What if this group is not working for us?

You're not alone! This could be the result of a personality conflict, life stage difference, geographical distance, level of spiritual maturity, or any number of things. Relax. Pray for God's direction, and at the end of this six-week study, decide whether to continue with this group or find another. You don't buy the first car you look at or marry the first person you date, and the same goes with a group. Don't bail out before the six weeks are up–God might have something to teach you. Also, don't run from conflict or prejudge people before you have given them a chance. God is still working in you too!

How do we handle the child care needs in our group?

We suggest that you empower the group to openly brainstorm solutions. You may try one option that works for a while and then adjust over time. Our favorite approach is for adults to meet in the living room or dining room and share the cost of a babysitter (or two) who can be with the kids in a different part of the house. In this way, parents don't have to be away from their children all evening when their children are too young to be left at home. A second option is to use one home for the kids and a second home (close by or a phone call away) for the adults. A third idea is to rotate the responsibility of providing a lesson or care for the children either in the same home or in another home nearby. This can be an incredible blessing for kids. Finally, the most common idea is to decide that you need to have a night to invest in your spiritual lives individually or as a couple, and to make your own arrangements for child care. No matter what decision the group makes, the best approach is to dialogue openly about both the problem and the solution.

SMALL GROUP AGREEMENT

Our Expectations:

To provide a predictable environment where participants experience authentic community and spiritual growth.

Group Attendance	We would like for everyone to make it a priority to attend each week.
Safe Environment	To help create a safe place where people can be heard and feel loved.
Respect Differences	To be gentle and gracious to fellow group members with different spiritual maturity, personal opinions, temperaments, or "imperfections." We are all works in progress.
Confidentiality	To keep anything that is shared strictly confidential and within the group, and to avoid sharing improper information about those outside the group.
Encouragement for Growth	To be not just takers but givers of life. We want to spiritually multiply our lives by serving others with our God-given gifts.
Shared Ownership	To remember that every member is a minister and to ensure that each attender will share a small team role or responsibility over time (i.e. bringing food or closing in prayer).
Rotating Hosts/ Leaders and Homes	To encourage different people to host the group in their homes, and to rotate the responsibility of facilitating each meeting (see the Small Group Calendar).

Our Times Together:

- Refreshments _____
- Childcare _____
- When we will meet (day of week) _____
- Where we will meet (place) _____
- We will begin at (time) _____ and end at _____
- We will do our best to have some or all of us attend a worship service together.
  Our primary worship service time will be _____

SMALL GROUP CALENDAR

Planning and calendaring can help ensure the greatest participation at every meeting. Be sure to include birthdays, socials, church events, holidays, and projects.

DATE	LESSON	HOST HOME	REFRESHMENTS	LEADER
MONDAY JAN 15	1	BILL	JOE	BILL

MEMORY VERSES

Week 1

Jesus answered, "It is written: 'Man does not live on bread alone, but on every word that comes from the mouth of God.'"
Matthew 4:4

Week 2

"Do you not know? Have you not heard? The LORD is the everlasting God, the Creator of the ends of the earth. He will not grow tired or weary, and his understanding no one can fathom."
Isaiah 40:28

Week 3

And we know that in all things God works for the good of those who love him, who have been called according to his purpose.
Romans 8:28

Week 4

"The Lord is my strength and my song; he has become my salvation. He is my God, and I will praise him, my father's God, and I will exalt him."
Exodus 15:2

Week 5

"Do not let this Book of the Law depart from your mouth; meditate on it day and night, so that you may be careful to do everything written in it. Then you will be prosperous and successful. ⁹ Have I not commanded you? Be strong and courageous. Do not be terrified; do not be discouraged, for the LORD your God will be with you wherever you go."
Joshua 1:8-9

Week 6

⁵ Trust in the LORD with all your heart and lean not on your own understanding; ⁶ in all your ways acknowledge him, and he will make your paths straight.
Proverbs 3:5-6

PRAYER AND PRAISE REPORT

THE **WHITEBOARD** BIBLE

	Prayer Requests	Praise Reports
Week 1		
Week 2		
Week 3		
Week 4		
Week 5		
Week 6		

One-Year Bible Reading Plan

Week 1
- ☐ Gen. 1-3
- ☐ Gen. 4-7
- ☐ Gen. 8-11
- ☐ Gen. 12-15
- ☐ Gen. 16-18
- ☐ Gen. 19-21
- ☐ Gen. 22-24

Week 2
- ☐ Gen. 25-26
- ☐ Gen. 27-29
- ☐ Gen. 30-31
- ☐ Gen. 32-34
- ☐ Gen. 35-37
- ☐ Gen. 38-40
- ☐ Gen. 41-42

Week 3
- ☐ Gen. 43-45
- ☐ Gen. 46-47
- ☐ Gen. 48-50
- ☐ Exod. 1-3
- ☐ Exod. 4-6
- ☐ Exod. 7-9
- ☐ Exod. 10-12

Week 4
- ☐ Exod. 13-15
- ☐ Exod. 16-18
- ☐ Exod. 19-21
- ☐ Exod. 22-24
- ☐ Exod. 25-27
- ☐ Exod. 28-29
- ☐ Exod. 30-32

Week 5
- ☐ Exod. 33-35
- ☐ Exod. 36-38
- ☐ Exod. 39-40
- ☐ Lev. 1-4
- ☐ Lev. 5-7
- ☐ Lev. 8-10
- ☐ Lev. 11-13

Week 6
- ☐ Lev. 14-15
- ☐ Lev. 16-17
- ☐ Lev. 18-19
- ☐ Lev. 20-21
- ☐ Lev. 22-23
- ☐ Lev. 24-25
- ☐ Lev. 26-27

Week 7
- ☐ Num. 1-4
- ☐ Num. 5-6
- ☐ Num. 7
- ☐ Num. 8-10
- ☐ Num. 11-13
- ☐ Num. 14-15
- ☐ Num. 16-17

Week 8
- ☐ Num. 18-20
- ☐ Num. 21-22
- ☐ Num. 23-25
- ☐ Num. 26-27
- ☐ Num. 28-30
- ☐ Num. 31-33
- ☐ Num. 34-36

Week 9
- ☐ Deut. 1
- ☐ Deut. 2
- ☐ Deut. 3-4
- ☐ Deut. 5-7
- ☐ Deut. 8-10
- ☐ Deut. 11-13
- ☐ Deut. 14-16

Week 10
- ☐ Deut. 17-19
- ☐ Deut. 20-22
- ☐ Deut. 23-25
- ☐ Deut. 26-27
- ☐ Deut. 28-30
- ☐ Deut. 31-32
- ☐ Deut. 33-34

Week 11
- ☐ Josh. 1-4
- ☐ Josh. 5-8
- ☐ Josh. 9-12
- ☐ Josh. 13-16
- ☐ Josh. 17-20
- ☐ Josh. 21-22
- ☐ Josh. 23-24

Week 12
- ☐ Judg. 1-4
- ☐ Judg. 5-7
- ☐ Judg. 8-10
- ☐ Judg. 11-14
- ☐ Judg. 15-18
- ☐ Judg. 19-21
- ☐ Ruth

Week 13
- ☐ 1 Sam. 1-4
- ☐ 1 Sam. 5-10
- ☐ 1 Sam. 11-14
- ☐ 1 Sam. 15-17
- ☐ 1 Sam. 18-21
- ☐ 1 Sam. 22-25
- ☐ 1 Sam. 26-31

Week 14
- ☐ 2 Sam. 1-4
- ☐ 2 Sam. 5-8
- ☐ 2 Sam. 9-12
- ☐ 2 Sam. 13-15
- ☐ 2 Sam. 16-18
- ☐ 2 Sam. 19-21
- ☐ 2 Sam. 22-24

Week 15
- ☐ 1 Kgs. 1-3
- ☐ 1 Kgs. 4-6
- ☐ 1 Kgs. 7-8
- ☐ 1 Kgs. 9-11
- ☐ 1 Kgs. 12-15
- ☐ 1 Kgs. 16-19
- ☐ 1 Kgs. 20-22

Week 16
- [ ] 2 Kgs. 1-4
- [ ] 2 Kgs. 5-8
- [ ] 2 Kgs. 9-11
- [ ] 2 Kgs. 12-15
- [ ] 2 Kgs. 16-18
- [ ] 2 Kgs. 19-22
- [ ] 2 Kgs. 23-25

Week 17
- [ ] 1 Chron. 1-2
- [ ] 1 Chron. 3-5
- [ ] 1 Chron. 6-7
- [ ] 1 Chron. 8-10
- [ ] 1 Chron. 11-17
- [ ] 1 Chron. 18-23
- [ ] 1 Chron. 24-26

Week 18
- [ ] 1 Chron. 27-29
- [ ] 2 Chron. 1-5
- [ ] 2 Chron. 6-9
- [ ] 2 Chron. 10-15
- [ ] 2 Chron. 16-20
- [ ] 2 Chron. 21-25
- [ ] 2 Chron. 26-29

Week 19
- [ ] 2 Chron. 30-32
- [ ] 2 Chron. 33-36
- [ ] Ezra 1-3
- [ ] Ezra 4-7
- [ ] Ezra 8-10
- [ ] Neh. 1-5
- [ ] Neh. 6-7

Week 20
- [ ] Neh. 8-10
- [ ] Neh. 11-13
- [ ] Est. 1-5
- [ ] Est. 6-10
- [ ] Job 1-5
- [ ] Job 6-9
- [ ] Job 10-13

Week 21
- [ ] Job 14-18
- [ ] Job 19-22
- [ ] Job 23-28
- [ ] Job 29-32
- [ ] Job 33-36
- [ ] Job 37-39
- [ ] Job 40-42

Week 22
- [ ] Ps. 1-9
- [ ] Ps. 10-17
- [ ] Ps. 18
- [ ] Ps. 19-22
- [ ] Ps. 23-29
- [ ] Ps. 30-34
- [ ] Ps. 35-39

Week 23
- [ ] Ps. 40-46
- [ ] Ps. 47-54
- [ ] Ps. 55-61
- [ ] Ps. 62-68
- [ ] Ps. 69-73
- [ ] Ps. 74-77
- [ ] Ps. 78-80

Week 24
- [ ] Ps. 81-87
- [ ] Ps. 88-91
- [ ] Ps. 92-100
- [ ] Ps. 101-104
- [ ] Ps. 105-106
- [ ] Ps. 107-110
- [ ] Ps. 111-118

Week 25
- [ ] Ps. 119:1-88
- [ ] Ps. 119:89-176
- [ ] Ps. 120-125
- [ ] Ps. 126-132
- [ ] Ps. 133-139
- [ ] Ps. 140-145
- [ ] Ps. 146-150

Week 26
- [ ] Prov. 1-3
- [ ] Prov. 4-6
- [ ] Prov. 7-10
- [ ] Prov. 11-14
- [ ] Prov. 15-17
- [ ] Prov. 18-20
- [ ] Prov. 21-23

Week 27
- [ ] Prov. 24-26
- [ ] Prov. 27-29
- [ ] Prov. 30-31
- [ ] Eccles. 1-4
- [ ] Eccles. 5-8
- [ ] Eccles. 9-12
- [ ] Song

Week 28
- [ ] Isa. 1-4
- [ ] Isa. 5-8
- [ ] Isa. 9-13
- [ ] Isa. 14-19
- [ ] Isa. 20-24
- [ ] Isa. 25-29
- [ ] Isa. 30-33

Week 29
- [ ] Isa. 34-37
- [ ] Isa. 38-41
- [ ] Isa. 42-45
- [ ] Isa. 46-51
- [ ] Isa. 52-57
- [ ] Isa. 58-61
- [ ] Isa. 62-66

Week 30
- [ ] Jer. 1-4
- [ ] Jer. 5-9
- [ ] Jer. 10-13
- [ ] Jer. 14-17
- [ ] Jer. 18-22
- [ ] Jer. 23-25
- [ ] Jer. 26-29

Week 31
- ☐ Jer. 30-31
- ☐ Jer. 32-34
- ☐ Jer. 35-37
- ☐ Jer. 38-41
- ☐ Jer. 42-45
- ☐ Jer. 46-48
- ☐ Jer. 49-52

Week 32
- ☐ Lam. 1-2
- ☐ Lam. 3-5
- ☐ Ezek. 1-2
- ☐ Ezek. 3-5
- ☐ Ezek. 6-8
- ☐ Ezek. 9-12
- ☐ Ezek. 13-15

Week 33
- ☐ Ezek. 16-17
- ☐ Ezek. 18-20
- ☐ Ezek. 21-22
- ☐ Ezek. 23-24
- ☐ Ezek. 25-27
- ☐ Ezek. 28-30
- ☐ Ezek. 31-33

Week 34
- ☐ Ezek. 34-36
- ☐ Ezek. 37-39
- ☐ Ezek. 40-42
- ☐ Ezek. 43-45
- ☐ Ezek. 46-48
- ☐ Dan. 1-3
- ☐ Dan. 4-6

Week 35
- ☐ Dan. 7-9
- ☐ Dan. 10-12
- ☐ Hos. 1-7
- ☐ Hos. 8-14
- ☐ Joel
- ☐ Amos 1-5
- ☐ Amos 6-9

Week 36
- ☐ Obad.-Jon.
- ☐ Mic.-Nah.
- ☐ Hab.-Zeph.
- ☐ Hag.
- ☐ Zech. 1-7
- ☐ Zech. 8-14
- ☐ Mal.

Week 37
- ☐ Matt. 1-2
- ☐ Matt. 3-4
- ☐ Matt. 5-6
- ☐ Matt. 7-8
- ☐ Matt. 9-10
- ☐ Matt. 11-12
- ☐ Matt. 13-14

Week 38
- ☐ Matt. 15-17
- ☐ Matt. 18-19
- ☐ Matt. 20-21
- ☐ Matt. 22-23
- ☐ Matt. 24-25
- ☐ Matt. 26
- ☐ Matt. 27-28

Week 39
- ☐ Mark 1-3
- ☐ Mark 4-5
- ☐ Mark 6-7
- ☐ Mark 8-9
- ☐ Mark 10-11
- ☐ Mark 12-14
- ☐ Mark 15-16

Week 40
- ☐ Luke 1
- ☐ Luke 2
- ☐ Luke 3
- ☐ Luke 4-5
- ☐ Luke 6-7
- ☐ Luke 8-9
- ☐ Luke 10-11

Week 41
- ☐ Luke 12-13
- ☐ Luke 14-15
- ☐ Luke 16
- ☐ Luke 17-18
- ☐ Luke 19-20
- ☐ Luke 21-22
- ☐ Luke 23-24

Week 42
- ☐ John 1-3
- ☐ John 4-7
- ☐ John 8-10
- ☐ John 11-13
- ☐ John 14-17
- ☐ John 18-19
- ☐ John 20-21

Week 43
- ☐ Acts 1-2
- ☐ Acts 3
- ☐ Acts 4-6
- ☐ Acts 7-8
- ☐ Acts 9-10
- ☐ Acts 11-13
- ☐ Acts 14-15

Week 44
- ☐ Acts 16-17
- ☐ Acts 18-20
- ☐ Acts 21-23
- ☐ Acts 24-26
- ☐ Acts 27-28
- ☐ Rom. 1-3
- ☐ Rom. 4-7

Week 45
- ☐ Rom. 8-10
- ☐ Rom. 11-13
- ☐ Rom. 14-16
- ☐ 1 Cor. 1-4
- ☐ 1 Cor. 5-8
- ☐ 1 Cor. 9-12
- ☐ 1 Cor. 13-16

Week 46
- ☐ 2 Cor. 1-3
- ☐ 2 Cor. 4-8
- ☐ 2 Cor. 9-11
- ☐ 2 Cor. 12-13
- ☐ Gal. 1-2
- ☐ Gal. 3-4
- ☐ Gal. 5-6

Week 47
- ☐ Eph.
- ☐ Phil.
- ☐ Col.
- ☐ 1 Thess.
- ☐ 2 Thess.
- ☐ 1 Tim.
- ☐ 2 Tim.

Week 48
- ☐ Titus - Philem.
- ☐ Heb. 1-6
- ☐ Heb. 7-10
- ☐ Heb. 11-13
- ☐ Jas.
- ☐ 1 Pet.
- ☐ 2 Pet.

Week 49
- ☐ 1 Jn. - 2 Jn.
- ☐ 3 Jn. - Jude
- ☐ Rev. 1-4
- ☐ Rev. 5-9
- ☐ Rev. 10-14
- ☐ Rev. 15-18
- ☐ Rev. 19-22

SMALL
GROUP
LEADERS

HOSTING AN OPEN HOUSE

If you're starting a new group, try planning an "open house" before your first formal group meeting. Even if you only have two to four core members, it's a great way to break the ice and to consider prayerfully who else might be open to joining you over the next few weeks. You can also use this kick-off meeting to hand out study guides, collect contact information for each person, ask for each person's birthday so you can later celebrate with them, spend some time getting to know each other, and briefly pray for each other.

A simple meal or good desserts always make a kick-off meeting more fun. After people introduce themselves and share how they ended up being at the meeting (you can play a game to see who has the wildest story!), have everyone respond to a few icebreaker questions: "What is your favorite family vacation?" or "What is one thing you love about your church/our community?" or "What are three things about your life growing up that most people here don't know?" Next, ask everyone to tell what he or she hopes to get out of the study. You might want to review the Small Group Agreement and talk about each person's expectations and priorities.

Finally, set an empty chair in the center of your group and explain that it represents someone who would enjoy or benefit from this group but who isn't here yet. Ask people to pray about whom they could invite to join the group over the next few weeks. Hand out postcards and have everyone write an invitation or two. Don't worry about ending up with too many people; you can always have one discussion circle in the living room and another in the dining room after you watch the lesson. Each group could then report prayer requests and progress at the end of the session.

You can skip this kick-off meeting if your time is limited, but you'll experience a huge benefit if you take the time to connect with each other in this way.

LEADING FOR THE FIRST TIME

- **Sweaty palms are a healthy sign.** The Bible says God is gracious to the humble. Remember who is in control; if you feel inadequate, that is probably a good sign. Those who are soft in heart (and sweaty palmed) are those through whom God is sure to speak.

- **Seek support.** Ask your leader, co-leader, or close friend to pray for you and prepare with you before the session. Walking through the study will help you anticipate potentially difficult questions and discussion topics.

- **Bring your uniqueness to the study.** Lean into who you are and how God wants you to uniquely lead the study.

- **Prepare.** Go through the lesson once before everyone arrives. Take time to listen to the teaching segment (DVD) and choose the questions you want to be sure to discuss.

- **Ask for feedback so you can grow.** Perhaps in an email or on cards handed out at the study, have everyone write down three things you did well and one thing you could improve on.

- **Share with your group what God is doing in your heart.** God is searching for those whose hearts are fully His. Share your trials and victories. We promise that people will relate.

- **One final challenge:** Before your first opportunity to lead, look up each of the five passages listed below. Read each one as a devotional exercise to help equip yourself with a shepherd's heart. Trust us on this one. If you do this, you will be more than ready for your first meeting.

Matthew 9:36
1 Peter 5:2-4
Psalm 23
Ezekiel 34:11-16
1 Thessalonians 2:7-8, 11-12

LEADERSHIP TRAINING 101

Congratulations! You have responded to the call to help shepherd Jesus' flock. There are few other tasks in the family of God that surpass the contribution you will be making. As you prepare to lead, whether it is one session or the entire series, here are a few thoughts to keep in mind. We encourage you to read these and review them with each new discussion leader before he or she leads.

1. **Ask God for help.** Pray right now for God to help you build a healthy group. If you can enlist a co-leader you will find your experience to be much richer.

2. **Just be yourself.** Use your unique gifts and temperament. Don't try to do things exactly like another leader; do them in a way that fits you!

3. **Prepare for your meeting ahead of time.** Review the session and the leader's notes, and write down your responses to each question. Pay special attention to exercises that ask group members to do something other than engage in discussion. Review "Outline for Each Session" so you'll remember the purpose of each section in the study.

4. **Pray for your group members by name.** Before you begin your session, go around the room in your mind and pray for each member by name. You may want to review the prayer list at least once a week. Ask God to use your time together to touch the heart of every person uniquely. Expect God to lead you to whomever He wants you to encourage or challenge in a special way. If you listen, God will surely lead!

5. **When you ask a question, be patient.** Someone will eventually respond. Sometimes people need a moment or two of silence to think about the question; if silence doesn't bother you, it won't bother anyone else. After someone responds, affirm the response with a simple "thanks" or "good point." Then ask, "How about somebody else?" or "Would someone who hasn't shared like to add anything?" Be sensitive to new people or reluctant members who aren't ready to say, pray, or do anything. If you give them a safe setting, they will blossom over time.

6   **Provide transitions between questions.** When guiding the discussion, use the "READ ALOUD" paragraphs as transitions into the questions. Ask the group if anyone would like to read the paragraph. Don't call on anyone, but ask for a volunteer, and then be patient until someone begins. Be sure to thank the person who reads aloud. These paragraphs can also be used for a more rich discussion if your group wants to expand on what was just read.

QUIZ ANSWER KEY

1. Who covered his hands and neck with goat skins to fool his father?
    a. Ichabod
    b. Joseph
    c. Jacob
    d. Nimrod

2. Which O.T. character married a Persian king?
    a. Ruth
    b. Esther
    c. Naomi
    d. Hannah

3. Who did God send to anoint Saul as King of Israel?
    a. Moses
    b. Joshua
    c. Eli
    d. Samuel

4. Who stole her father's idols and hid them in the saddle of her camel?
    a. Leah
    b. Rachel
    c. Deborah
    d. Rebekah

5. Who killed his brother while they were in the fields?
    a. Cain
    b. Jonathon
    c. Moses
    d. Elisha

6. Who led the Israelites into the Promised Land?
    a. Moses
    b. Joseph
    c. Jesus
    d. Joshua

7. Who fled from Sodom and Gomorrah before destruction came?
    a. Gomer
    b. Saul
    c. Lot
    d. Less

8. Who was told to build an ark before a flood covered the earth?

a. Moses
b. Jonah
c. Noah
d. Abraham

9. Which king went to the witch of Endor for assistance?

a. Hezekiah
b. Melchizidek
c. Solomon
d. Saul

10. How many animals did Moses take on the ark?

a. 2 of each kind
b. 7 pairs of clean animals
c. All of the above
d. None of the above

11. Who built the Second Temple?

a. Zerubbabel
b. Solomon
c. Herod
d. David

12. Which O.T. character interpreted Nebuchadnezzar's dream?

a. Isaiah
b. Jeremiah
c. Zedekiah
d. Daniel

13. Where did Cornelius live when Peter visited his home?

a. Smyrna
b. Jerusalem
c. Joppa
d. Caesarea

14. What was Timothy's home town?

a. Jerusalem
b. Ephesus
c. Lystra
d. Phillipi

PASTOR ALLEN JACKSON

Allen Jackson is passionate about helping people become more fully devoted followers of Jesus Christ who respond to God's invitations for their life.

He has served World Outreach Church since 1981, becoming senior pastor in 1989. Under his leadership, WOC has grown to a congregation of over 15,000 through outreach activities, community events and worship services designed to share the Gospel.

Through Allen Jackson Ministries, his messages reach people across the globe — through television, radio, Sirius XM, and online streaming. His teachings are also available in published books and other resources. Jackson has spoken at pastors' conferences in the U.S. and abroad, and has been a featured speaker during Jerusalem's Feast of Tabernacles celebration for the Vision for Israel organization and the International Christian Embassy-Jerusalem. Allen Jackson Ministries coaches pastors around the world, writing and publishing small-group curriculum used in states across the US, as well as Israel, Guatemala, the Philippines, Bermuda, Mexico, the United Kingdom, and South Africa.

With degrees from Oral Roberts University and Vanderbilt University, and additional studies at Gordon-Conwell Theological Seminary and Hebrew University of Jerusalem, Jackson is uniquely equipped to help people develop a love and understanding of God's Word.

Pastor Jackson's wife, Kathy, is an active participant in ministry at World Outreach Church.

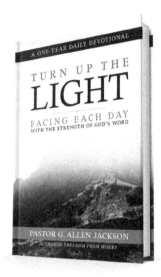

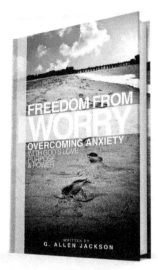

For more from Allen Jackson—including sermons, books, and small group materials—visit:

allenjackson.com

CPSIA information can be obtained
at www.ICGtesting.com
Printed in the USA
LVHW062059230121
677257LV00001B/2